This book belongs to:

Distributed by Diverse Dimensions, LLC
Illustration by FolksnFables
(Team: Neethi Joseph, Jumana VP, Indu Shaji)

978-1-7379987-6-1 (Paperback)
978-1-7379987-0-9 (Hardback)

Dedication

This book is dedicated to the children who want to reach for the stars both in their imagination and the manifestations of their lives.

About the author

The author, Carolyn Furlow, has a Master of Arts degree, in Creative Writing, A Bachelor of Science in Interdisciplinary Studies and a double minor in Psychology Afro American studies.

She is the mother of three adult children and a grandmother to one darling granddaughter, Imani. As a teacher, she has experienced first-hand the faces of isolation on students who feel disconnected to the lessons and reading materials in their classrooms. In a spirit of love and high regard for all children, she and her daughter, Amelia Furlow, have created a series of stories which speaks to all children and allows them to feel connected to the stories they read in classrooms and at home. The world is a visible melting pot of beautiful children across the globe. Our stories reflect their presence and fosters acceptance and respect.

About the author

The author, Amelia Furlow is currently a Marriage and Therapy Family Intern with a specialization in Trauma Studies. She received her Bachelor of Arts in Afro-American Studies from California State University, Los Angeles.

Amelia saw a need for more diverse stories to be told within children's books. She collaborated with her mother, Carolyn Furlow, to create a series of children's books that highlight the similarities as well as the individuality of being human. Telling stories that celebrate one's uniqueness and sameness allows children to embrace the skin they are in. Having grown up in Los Angeles, California, Texas, and Chesapeake Beach, Maryland, Amelia experienced the power of diversity at a very young age. Today, more than ever, children need to feel included. This series not only offers inclusiveness, it brings cheer to those who read it!

www.ingramcontent.com/pod-product-compliance
Lightning Source LLC
Chambersburg PA
CBHW080633030426

42336CB00018B/3188